A guide to the stock market & investing

A GUIDE TO THE STOCK MARKET &
INVESTING

Written by Babak Parvizi

A guide to the stock market & investing provides you all the necessary information about how to invest, how those shares work and that they are, where to invest in, what your investment duration could be, different investment products like stocks , bonds and turbo's, how to analyze stocks by graph and by actual figures.

Table of content

Introduction

Dear reader, during 8 years of study at the university, investing in my free time and during my work at a bank I made the decision to write a practical handbook for young and older people on how to invest. So that they will not make the same mistakes as I did and have the opportunity to make a profit out of their investment. Although I would like to warn you in all the honesty that with investing in the stock market you could gain a lot of profit but also lose money. Of course there are different strategies and ways to reduce the risk by being smart and by using different techniques.

A person can invest in the market for many different reasons and invest in different investment tools with different risks/profits. Some people may invest to gain more wealth so that they could have a comfortable life, go on vacation and buy whatever they want in a short term. Some invest to for a growth of wealth so that they could have a comfortable pension, and when they reach the age to retire. They would like to have a steady income rather than to take more risk. I hope that after reading this book you would have the different tools and knowledge so that you could start investing. It does not matter for which reason you do it, I sincerely believe that everybody should have a comfortable and enjoyable life. Because of the crisis, unemployment and government cutting on retirement plans people are more reluctant to take their future in own hands and make the best they can make of. Are you that person? Than I wish you good luck and much pleasure in the road to wealth and freedom. Because from now on your future is in your hands!

About the author

A long time ago a life of a young man started in the middle east. He was born in a Persian state, grown in a middle class family. The family were religious with strong norms and values, but it didn't matter how hard they tried the dictatorial government had put pressure on households by extreme political measure and by a weakened economy due to many reasons like mismanagement of the economical department and decisions. This family flee away because of economical disturbance in the 90's to a small European country. The young man grew and got older, as he got older he got interested in savings, interest and different interest rates in different countries. For example, if you put your money in a savings account in Germany, you would get a return on investment (ROI) on your savings account of 2%. But if you put your money in a savings account in lets say china, you would get 7%. But on the other hand if the currency of China devalues by 5,5 % that year, you will have a ROI of 1,5% which is lower than in Germany. So the young man started to read books about investing and different investment strategies. As he got to the point of going to the university, he made the decision to study international economics and business. During his study he invested in different companies with many gains and some losses. His losses were due his impatience, because these were actual good investments, but as I said earlier. It is important to choose your investment duration so that you could use different strategies and tools. He graduated from the university, started working in a bank and later on other companies and also started his own firm in accounting and consulting. But in all those years in his life, he made the chose to make his own choices in life and live the life he wanted. Which was a good decent life bound by norms and ethical values. And improve life quality on different aspects like health trough sporting, wealth by working, learning, saving, investing and entrepreneurship.

What is investing

We first have to start understanding what investing means and different ways to invest. Investing means using your (accumulated) wealth in different products/companies in the hope that those products gain in price. Well for which reason does a product gain in price? When a there is a high demand in a certain product and less offers the price will be higher that a product which has a low demand with a lot of producers/sellers and offers. We could use an example, strawberries usually grow in the summer. Which means that many tailors will produce strawberries and you will have a high quantity of offers at the market. Lets say that a small box of strawberries will cost 1 Euro equivalent to 1,4 dollars at the currency rate in 2014. In the winter the strawberries are usually sold out, a proportion will rot and the rest which was plucked in the beginning of the winter will be less in terms of quantity. When you go to the same market in the winter you will see that there are less sales people selling those strawberries. But the usual household would like to purchase the same amount of strawberries. Which will mean that due to weather conditions those strawberries will be harder to produce. The price of a small box of strawberries will be 1,95 Euro or higher. And the salesman will actually sell those products for that price. When this economic model counts for a pack of goods or fruit it also counts for the stock market and real estate price. Even when the company doesn't have the good business model, if there is a high speculation and need for those stocks because people believe in that company, it will still gain value.

In the past our grandparents would save money and keep this in old socks, which is partially true if I look at my own grandmother. But nowadays you could save that money or even borrow it and put it in a place where people need it. What does that mean? Some companies want to expand, or purchase new machines. In order to make to investments they need capita. The capital could be financed by different ways, the company could borrow money from the bank and pay a certain amount of interest or they could issue stocks. Where small and big investors like pension funds will purchase their stocks and gain a piece in that company. The company then has the ability to purchase different machineries to produce more and expand which could lead to higher returns. And that return will theoretically be recalculated in a higher stock price. When you sell that higher stock price in the future, it will have a higher value than your original investment.

Different investments products
Below I will explain different tools wealthy people use to accumulate more wealth.
Stocks
Stocks are a piece of a company, lets say the company has 1000 dollars worth of machines, a brand that is not known by many and is worth 500 dollars. On the bank account of the company there is 500 dollars and they have a small loan worth 300 dollars which was needed for purchasing those machines. The total amount which the company is worth is 1000+500+500-300= 1700 dollars. Lets say that the company has 1 owner which did not spend any penny on the company but many shareholders. The virtual company will have 17 share holders, each shareholder invested 100 dollars in the company in the hope to gain more wealth. When the company wants to expand they will issue new stocks, lets say that they need another 300 dollars for a machine. They will therefore issue 3 other stocks on the stock market which I will explain later on. You as a investor will contact your bank and buy 3 stocks each worth 100 dollars. If the company gains a higher profit in the future and many other people want to purchase the same stocks, they will call their bank, or make a electronic transaction trough internet banking and purchase your stocks if you want to cash in. The computers at the stock market will calculate that the share price will be worth 150 dollars each for the good profits of the company and the high demand. You will therefore make 3x50 dollar (profit)= 150 dollar profit on a investment of 300 dollar which is 50%. The stocks, and prices are listed on the stock market. Each country has a stock market and it is

possible to invest in a stock market in a different country, you usually need a currency bank account or a separate abroad stock account. In the US there are different stock exchanges, the biggest is NYSE, which is called New York stock exchange. And the smaller companies have a rating on another exchange list called the S&P. In the Netherlands the biggest companies are listed on the AEX, all the stock prices which are listed on that are calculated. The AEX has also a rating made trough all those stock prices, It is currently rated on 413 Euro. But that still means that if you want to buy a share in Shell, it will cost you 23 dollars per piece and not 413. In the past you got a piece of paper written on it how much shares you have in that company. But now the purchase and sales of those stocks are now done virtually by computer calculations, and you will see the amount of shares and price per share digitally on your internet bank account. Usually you have to pay the bank a small fee of lets say 3 dollars if you want to buy those stocks. You have to pay that fee for their service, because as a small investor you are not able to purchase stocks directly on the stock exchange, but you will do this trough your bank or broker. Your broker will spend time to buy those shares and settle it on your bank account. You can buy stocks even when you have 100 dollars, but it will be wise to start with a minimum amount of 1000 dollars. The reason for that is that have to pay the bank a fee of 3 Euro for their service which means that it counts for 3 percent profits if you buy for 100 Euros.

Bonds

Bonds are a piece of paper stating that the company owes you. When a company or government wants to borrow money they can issue bonds, usually worth 1000 dollars each and pay interest on that. The interest is made trough the credit rating. If the company has a low liquidity, low savings, bad product and is not well known the rating agencies give a low rating like C, which means that you will get a higher interest, lets say 8%. But this also means that you are willing to take higher risks. Those bonds are also listed on the bond exchange. On the issuing date each bond price is 1000 dollars worth, with a interest rate of lets say 5%. But is the demand will be low in the future due to higher risks which will be said on the news, the bond price could decline and the interest rate therefore has to increase to attract investors. Some investors purchase those bonds and keep them till maturity date, which is the end date of those bonds, that could be 1 year or 10 years. But some purchase those bonds when it is economically going bad with the company, the bond price is then low with a high interest rate. But they keep that bond for a short while and sell it when the company gives good news about higher profits they earned and for example low interest rates of the savings account. Then it is more attracting to invest in that bond price, and while many people want to buy those bonds instead of keeping their money on a low savings account. The short term investor will sell his bonds for a higher price.

Leverage products like options, turbos and sprinters
Leverage products are products made by the banks,
but are linked to for example a stock. Lets say that the
shares of Shell cost 20 Euros each, the turbo or
printer linked to that stock costs 5 Euros. Which
means that this has a leverage of 4. A leverage means
that you only pay 4 Euros and your bank pays 16
Euros. You will may have to pay a automatic fee of
for example 1% interest rate to the bank for that 16
Euros which will be a few cents. So if the stock price
grows up with 4 Euros. The stock price will be 24
Euros, which is a increase of 20%. But if you
purchased a turbo with a leverage of 4 it means that
you paid 5 Euros and you will get the full profit of 4
Euro increase in price= 9 Euros. But you paid just 5
Euros, and you gains 4. Which means that you have a
return of 80%. You can invest smaller amounts and
make higher profits, but also lose much more because
of the leverage. You could also put a automated
stop/loss on your shares which means that the banker
will sell your turbo's at lets say when the stock price
decreases to 18 Euros instead of 20. Your 5 Euros
will be worth 3 Euros. And the bank will sell the
stocks for you automatically, it is still better to lose 2
Euros in stead of the full amount.

Dividend

What is dividend? Dividend is when the company makes profits, it keeps a part of the profits and pays the rest to its shareholders. Lets say the company want to pay 100 Euros and the company issues 100 shares. This means that each share which could be 20 Euros will have a dividend payment of 1 Euro of profits. This means that you make 5% (1euro is 5% profits on a share price of 20 Euros) profit by doing nothing and only getting a part of the profits. The dividend payment is separate from the stock exchange price, which means that you can get a profit when the stock exchange price increases but also earn money buy receiving a part of the profits by cash. The dividend payment differs per company, some pay none, some pay 4 times a year. The companies who pay out dividend could pay this pay money or by shares. Which means that if you get 1 Euro dividend on a share price of 20. You will have 1, 05 shares. If yous ell those shares in the future then you will still have 21 Euros. 20X 1,05= 21 Euros.

Why are those dividend payments important! If you are retired and you want to have a added income on your retirement plan, you don't want to sell your shares every 3 months. You rather buy shares of a company which pays out 4x a year dividends in cash. Which means that every 3 months you will get a certain amount of money no matter how the company share price is listed and if there are low demand for that share. You will still have a quarterly added income. Thats why it is important to know that the reason is which you are investing for.

Investment period & duration

The investment period and duration has to do with how long you are willing to keep your investment products without needing to sell it. You have to understand that except the speculators on the stockmarket, the average investor should invest the money he or she does not need. Otherwise if you purchase a stock and the stock plumbs for a short period of time due to negative macro economic reasons then if you need your money you will need to sell your stocks with a loss. Otherwise you could have waited till the economic situation improves. If you want to invest for a long time for example for the reason of having a comfortable quarterly dividend payment in your retirement you should not take too many risk. But on the other hand if you are you and have a long period till your retirement you have a long investment duration. This is also linked to the willingness to take risks. In this case you could take more risk than a person who is 62 years old on the edge of retirement and needs his savings for a stable income. This person needs to put his money in a safe investment vehicle, for example 5 year investment bond.

Risk

As I mentioned above, the investment period is very important to know how much risk you are willing to take. On average a long investment period >10 years is willing to take more risk. But a person with a investment period of <8 years, for example 3 years is less likely to take risks. Because the stock market can crash and if you need your saving then you have to sell your stocks for a miserable price.

If you are willing to have higher returns but also willing to take higher losses, then you rather purchase 20% bonds and 60%stocks and 20% derivatives, real estate paper and commodities. If you are willing to take less risk it will be vice versa. It will be safer to purchase 60% bonds, put 20% on a savings account and purchase 20% stocks with low volatility. I have to say that these are average numbers, and losses made by each person is the responsibility of that person itself. These measures are mostly used by bank investment advisors and these figures changes as the economic outlook changes. When the economy is not stable, the investment advisors advice to put more in a savings account in case that a good opportunity comes by to invest in and take less risk.

Spreading risk and diversifying

When you want to invest or purchase stocks it would be smart to diversify your investment and risk. What does that mean? This is not the case if you only have a small amount of 1000 dollars to invest. Lets say you have high savings due to bonuses and inheritances which will sum up to 1 million dollar. It would not be wise for you to put all your savings in to 1 stock or company. You rather diversify your investment in case that a sector or country does not perform well. In the case that you are living in the US and have a investment time of 20 years and 1 million dollars you would spread in this way or approximately something alike:

Region
55% North and South America
20% Europe
15% Asia
10% Africa

If you are willing to take some risks
Products
30% Stocks
45% Funds
15% Bonds
10% Derivatives and Real estate papers/fund

70% growth stocks and 30% payment stocks, the growth stocks have a higher beta(beta= risk) and will more likely increase/decrease higher in value than stocks who are traditional like Shell and pay high dividends.

This is a pie chart so you could see a example and the difference between a aggressive portfolio who is willing to take more risks, with more stocks than bonds. In a conservative portfolio you will have more bonds due to steady payment :

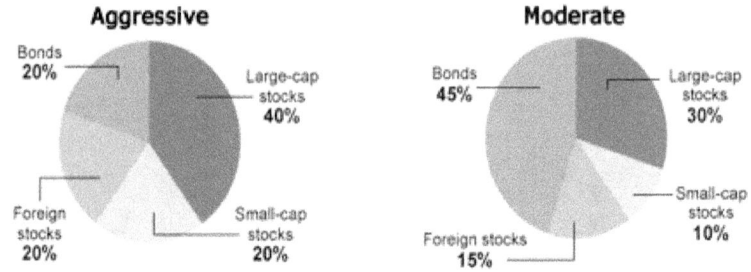

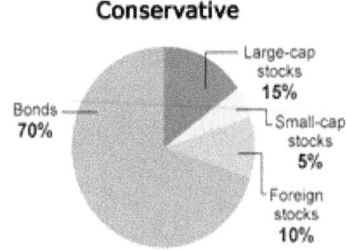

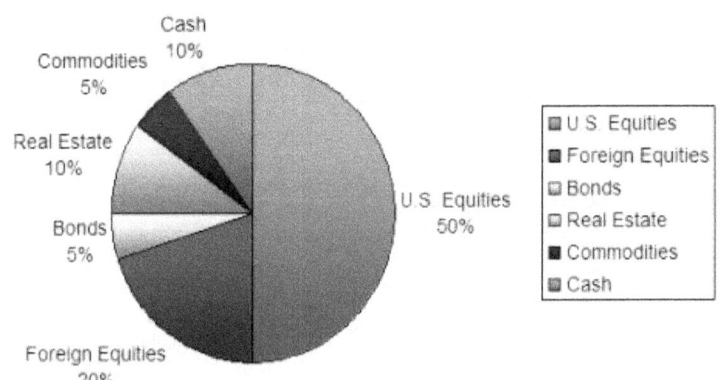

In the graph below you could see for example that a aggressive portfolio of a young person between 25 and 50 would purchase more stocks (green color). And a conservative person between 60 and 65 year old will have more bonds (grey color) than stocks.

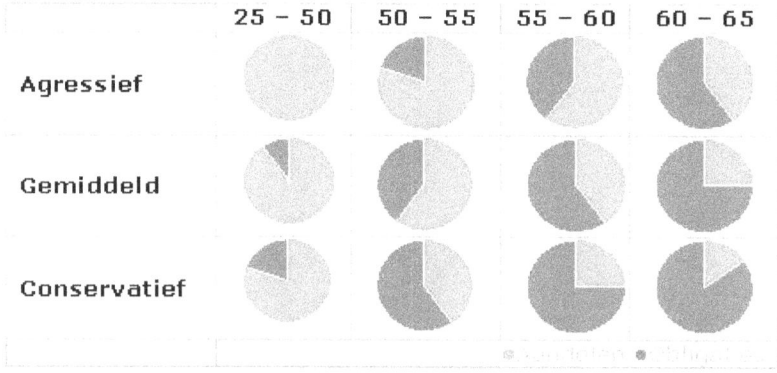

In the graph below you will see the diversification per region, some countries have more investment risk due to economic or political turbulence like the middle east between 2009 and 2014. It will be wise for you to invest most of your money in America and Europe, also because of a strong currency.

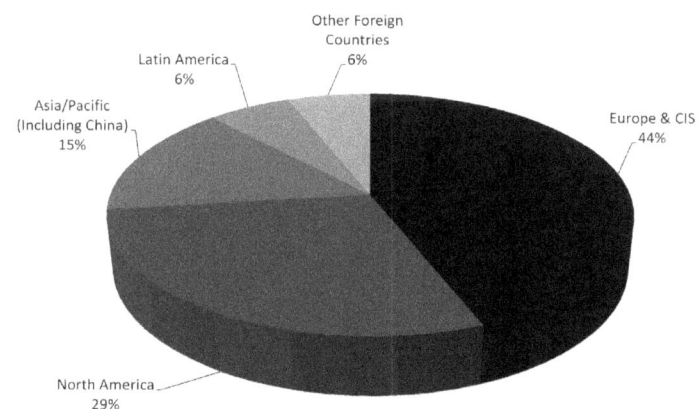

In this graph below you see in which sectors you could invest in. During the credit crisis the financial sector underperformed. Under performance is still a soft word for the catastrophe which came in to effect when the banks like Lehman Brothers fell. It would therefore be wise to purchase stocks in consumer goods, food, financials, IT sector, health care and real estate.

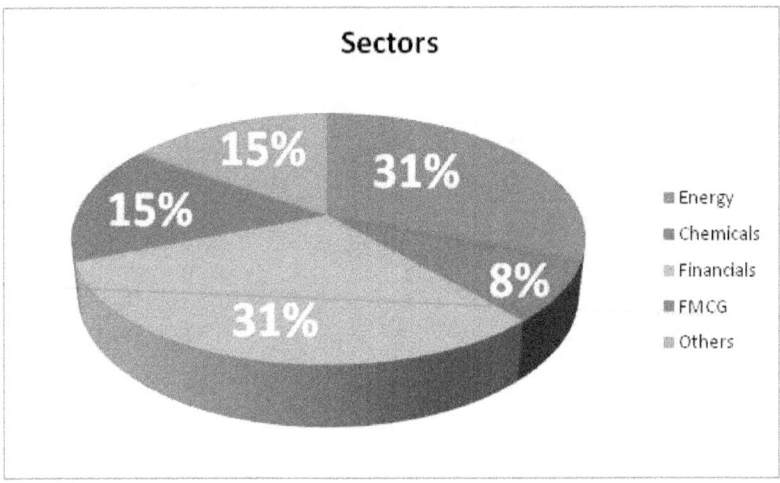

Finally in the graph below you will see different stocks, this is of course just an example of some stocks where investors invest in. Although the figures are fictive and it would not be wise to put 19 percent of your portfolio in 1 stock.

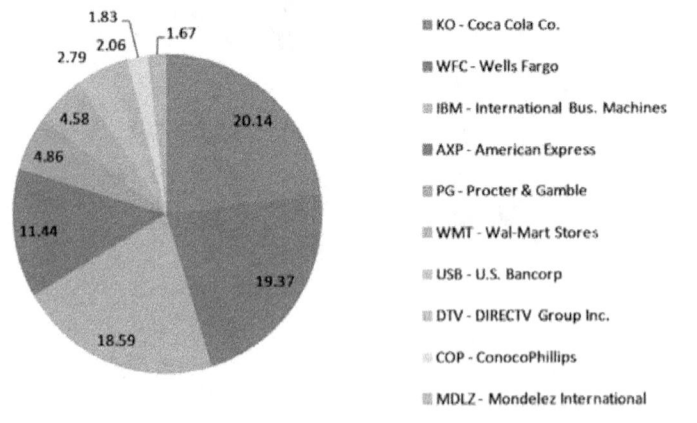

How do you choose the stocks

You can choose the stocks with different methods. But I would like to explain a actual research done about stock picking. The researchers let a group of professional investors choose stocks and a monkey playfully choose his stocks. The results were astonishing. On a small time frame the monkey outperformed the actual professional investors with higher returns!

There are 2 ways to analyze stocks, this is on the basis of technical analysis and fundamental analysis. With technical analysis you choose the stocks based on graphical performance in the past and forecasts of the future. If you choose fundamental analysis you rather focus on the macro-economical and micro-economical factors of the company and the economy.

Fundamental analysis
With fundamental analysis you look at the micro-economical and macro-economical factors. Micro economical factors include the revenue and revenue growth of the company, you can find this on their web site under the topic about or investor relations. You have to also analyze the macro economic factors these include global economy, country, political en product segment. You will analyze:

*industry analysis
*company analysis like
*revenue
*the business performance
*the credit risk
*liquidity
*revenue growth per year
*dividend
*net profit
*profit margin
*assets
*expenses
*dept
*p/e ratio
*the management performance

You will have to look at the balance sheet and income statement of the company to see the actual figures. When the company has only high revenues but also a high dept and almost no net profits, the company is not a profitable company. It is merely breaking even and making up the costs. But when the company has even lower figures but no dept and a high profit margin and high net income with much savings. Then this company would be a more profitable company to invest in. They could even use their savings to expand. You could also compare a few years of performance, to see if there is a increase of revenue or a lower revenue and increase of dept which could be bad for the company except if it was because they wanted to expand and invest.

Technical analysis

Technical analysis maintains that all information is reflected already in the stock price. Trends are your friend and sentiment changes predate and predict trend changes. Investors emotional responses to price movements lead to recognizable price chart patterns. Technical analysis does not care what the value of a stock is. Their price predictions are only extrapolations from historical price patterns. Just as there are many investment styles on the fundamental side, there are also many different types of technical traders. Some rely on chart patterns, others use technical indicators and oscillators, and most use some combination of the two. Either way, technical analysts it's exclusive use of historical price and volume data is what separates them from their fundamental counterparts. Unlike fundamental analysts, technical analysts don't care whether a stock is undervalued. The only thing that matters is a stock's past trading data and what information this data can provide about where the security might move in the future. If the stock price always went up, it could be a good indicator, but it can also mean that there is a bubble which has to be yet revealed. But the critics say that it only includes price movements and doesn't take in to account the fundamental factors of the company which are actual performance.

With technical analysis you will analyze the following:

*price moves in trends

*if historical trends repeats itself

*is the stock over or undervalued

In the graph below you will see a uptrend

In technical analysis, it is the movement of the highs and lows that constitutes a trend. For example, an uptrend is classified as a series of higher highs and higher lows, while a downtrend is one of lower lows and lower highs. If after the low 1 the stock price increases but then falls lower than 1 it will mean that it will have to take more effort to reach the past high performance because there will be a resistant line at low 1.

In this graph you see a side way trend, this is handy for short term investors. Even daily traders use this to see there they have to but and to sell the stock to make a profit.

There are different type of charts which you can use online or at your investment account. Some use bar charts and some use line charts. I prefer a line chart but many investors prefer a bar chart or candlesticks.

In the graph below you see a example of a candlestick.

When you see a chart pattern it gives you a trading signal. Either to sell or to buy or to hold. For example if you had a double bottom in the graph below it is most likely that the chart is going up in the near future.

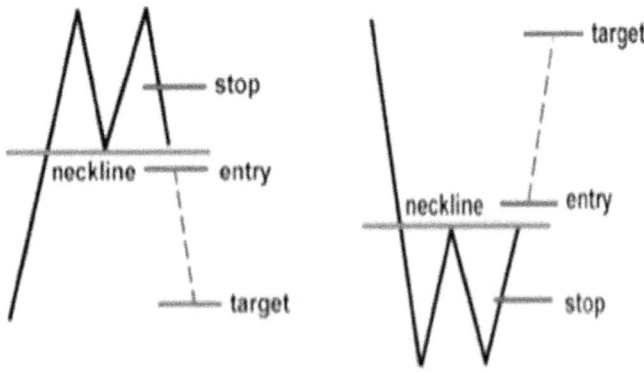

Double Top and Double Bottom

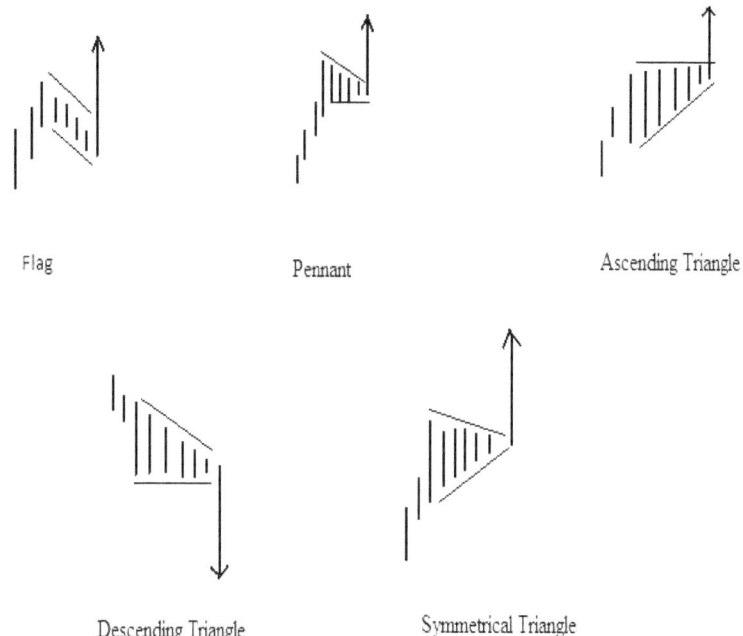

Flag

Pennant

Ascending Triangle

Descending Triangle

Symmetrical Triangle

These are some tools investors use to make investment decisions. You can try and use and create your own strategy. What works for you may not work for me. In the Past I have made with a single trade within a few weeks 52% profit with no leverage, if it was a leverage 3 like a turbo long then I would had 156% on profits. Practice with small amounts or virtual trading platforms are the best.

Thank you word

I hope this book provided you with all the necessary basic information about stocks and investing. You could always read more in depth about different things which I mentioned in this book. A wise man once said that a person with low self esteem tries and falls and never tries again. A person with a high self esteem is so persistent that he will try till he finally does not get defeated. And I did not mention winning, but not being defeated! I wish you good luck, enjoyment and wealth in the future.

www.ingramcontent.com/pod-product-compliance
Lightning Source LLC
Chambersburg PA
CBHW070757180526
45168CB00004B/1657